SIDNEY CROSBY
Hockey Superstar

BY MATT DOEDEN

CAPSTONE PRESS

a capstone imprint

Sports Illustrated KIDS Superstar Athletes is published by Capstone Press,
1710 Roe Crest Drive, North Mankato, Minnesota 56003.
www.capstonepub.com

Sports Illustrated Kids is a trademark of Time Inc. Used with permission.

 Books published by Capstone Press are manufactured with paper
containing at least 10 percent post-consumer waste.

Library of Congress Cataloging-in-Publication Data
Doeden, Matt.
  Sidney Crosby : hockey superstar / by Matt Doeden.
    p. cm. — (Sports illustrated kids: superstar athletes)
  Includes bibliographical references and index.
  Summary: "Presents the athletic biography of Sidney Crosby, including his career as a high school and
professional hockey player"—Provided by publisher.
  ISBN 978-1-4296-7684-7 (library binding)
  ISBN 978-1-4296-8005-9 (paperback)
  1. Crosby, Sidney, 1987– —Juvenile literature. 2. Hockey players—Canada—Biography—Juvenile
literature. I. Title. II. Series.
  GV848.5.C76D64 2012
  796.962092--dc23   2011034032

Editorial Credits
Angie Kaelberer, editor; Ted Williams, designer; Eric Gohl, media researcher;
    Laura Manthe, production specialist

Photo Credits
Courtesy of Shattuck-St. Mary's/Paul Swenson Photography, 10
Newscom/RTR/Chris Wattie, 13
Sports Illustrated/Damian Strohmeyer, 5; David E. Klutho, cover (all), 1,
    2–3, 7, 9, 15, 16, 17, 19, 21, 22 (top & bottom), 23, 24; Robert Beck, 6, 22 (middle)

Design Elements
Shutterstock/chudo-yudo, designerpix, Fassver Anna, Fazakas Mihaly

Direct Quotations
Page 7, from March 1, 2010, ESPN.com, "Crosby beats Miller in OT to earn gold for Canada, end
    U.S. run," www.sports.espn.go.com
Page 12, from September 9, 2005, Associated Press article, "Crosby Signs," www.sportsillustrated.cnn.com
Page 18, from December 31, 2010, *USA Today* article, "Penguins superstar Sidney Crosby keeps raising
    game," by Kevin Allen, www.usatoday.com

Printed in the United States of America in North Mankato, Minnesota.
102011   006405CGS12

TABLE OF CONTENTS

CHAPTER 1

OLYMPIC HERO

It was overtime of the 2010 Olympic gold-medal game in men's hockey. The United States and Canada were tied 2-2. The next goal would win the gold.

Players sped up and down the ice. The goaltenders stopped shot after shot. Then Canada **center** Sidney Crosby got the puck. He fired a shot. But U.S. goaltender Ryan Miller blocked it.

center—a player whose main job is to play in the middle of the ice, away from the side boards

The puck bounced to Miller's right. Crosby quickly retrieved it. He passed to teammate Jarome Iginla. Iginla passed it back as Crosby streaked toward the goal. He whipped a quick shot past Miller. Crosby had won the gold medal for Canada.

"It's a pretty unbelievable thing, you dream of that a thousand times growing up. For it to come true is amazing."—Sidney Crosby

CHAPTER 2

BORN TO SKATE

Sidney Patrick Crosby always wanted to be a hockey player. He was born August 7, 1987, in Cole Harbour, Nova Scotia, Canada. He started shooting pucks in his basement at age 2. The family's washing machine had dents from all the shots. Crosby could skate by the time he was 3.

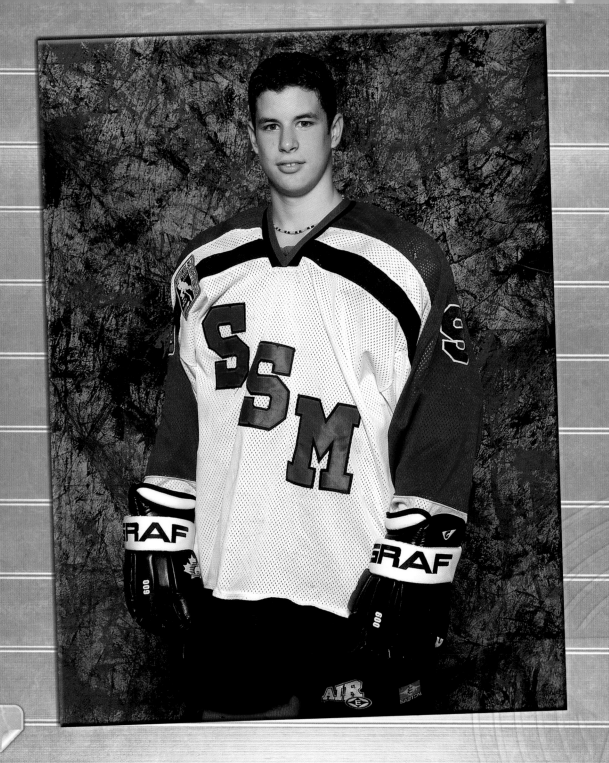

Crosby was a natural on the ice. At age 9 he scored 159 goals in just 55 games. By age 14 he was famous across Canada. Coaches and reporters said his skills were far above those of kids his age.

Many fans said Crosby would be the next Wayne Gretzky. Gretzky is considered to be the greatest player in NHL history.

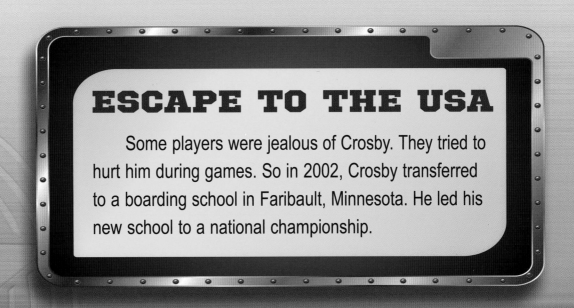

ESCAPE TO THE USA

Some players were jealous of Crosby. They tried to hurt him during games. So in 2002, Crosby transferred to a boarding school in Faribault, Minnesota. He led his new school to a national championship.

In 2003 Crosby joined the Rimouski Oceanic of the Quebec Major Junior Hockey League (QMJHL). In the 2004–2005 season, he scored 168 **points** in just 62 games.

The Pittsburgh Penguins had the first pick in the 2005 NHL **draft**. They chose Crosby, who was just 17 years old.

points—a player's total goals plus assists
draft—the process of choosing a person to join a sports team

"Obviously, this is a new level. But the pressure has always been there. I've always put a lot of pressure on myself to perform."—Sidney Crosby, on joining the NHL

CHAPTER 3

NHL STAR

Crosby was only 18 when he joined the Penguins. He was an instant star. He had 39 goals and 63 assists as a **rookie**. The next year he led the NHL with 120 points.

In 2007–2008 Crosby missed 29 games with an ankle injury. But he was healthy for the playoffs. He had 6 goals and 21 assists in 20 playoff games. The Penguins reached the Stanley Cup Finals. But they lost to the Detroit Red Wings.

rookie—a first-year player

Crosby led the Penguins back to the Finals in 2008–2009. The Penguins again faced the Red Wings. Detroit won the first two games. But the Penguins fought back. Crosby scored a goal in Game 4 to tie the series 2-2.

The series remained tied after the teams split the next two games. In the final game Crosby hurt his knee in the second period. He missed the rest of the game. But the Penguins still won 2-1. They were Stanley Cup champions!

Crosby dominated in 2009–2010. He led the NHL with 51 goals. In February 2010, he helped Canada win the Olympic gold medal. In 2011 Crosby was among the league-leaders in goals until he suffered a **concussion**. He was out for the rest of the season.

concussion—an injury to the brain caused by a hard blow to the head

"I just try to make sure I get the shot off as quick as possible to catch goalies off guard."—Sidney Crosby

CHAPTER 4

A SPECIAL PLAYER

Crosby is a rare talent. He's a fast, smooth skater. His shot combines power with an accurate touch. He seems to sense where teammates and opponents are without even looking. Many hockey experts think he could be one of the game's all-time greats. They say he's not the next Wayne Gretzky, but the first Sidney Crosby.

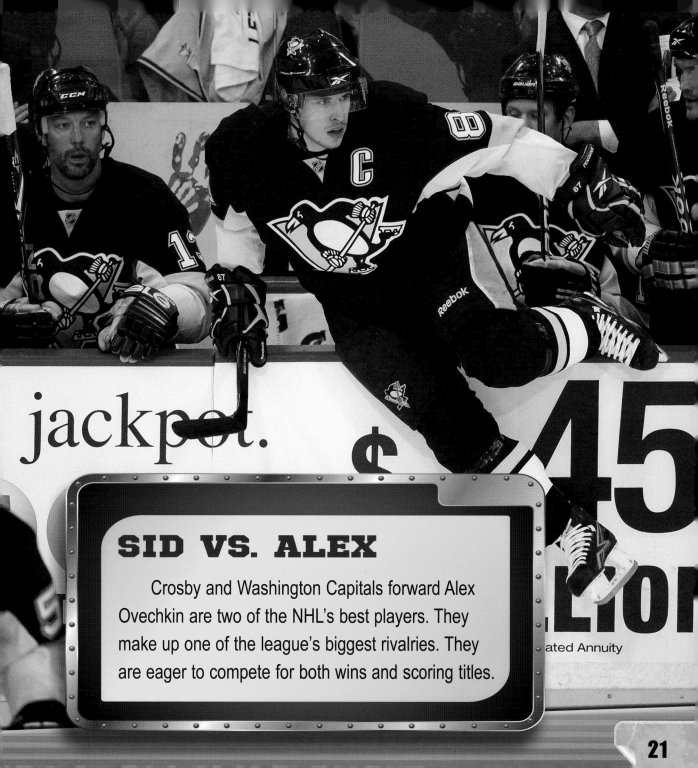

SID VS. ALEX

Crosby and Washington Capitals forward Alex Ovechkin are two of the NHL's best players. They make up one of the league's biggest rivalries. They are eager to compete for both wins and scoring titles.

TIMELINE

1987—Sidney Patrick Crosby is born August 7, 1987, in Cole Harbour, Nova Scotia, Canada.

2002—Crosby leads Shattuck-St. Mary's prep school team to a national championship.

2003—Crosby joins the Rimouski Oceanic of the QMJHL.

2005—The Pittsburgh Penguins choose Crosby with the No. 1 pick in the NHL draft.

2009—The Penguins beat the Red Wings in the Finals to become Stanley Cup Champions.

2010—Crosby scores the gold-medal-winning goal at the Winter Olympics. He also leads the NHL in goals.

2011—Crosby suffers a concussion that forces him to miss the second half of the season.

GLOSSARY

assist (uh-SIST)—a pass that leads to a score by a teammate

center (SEN-tur)—a player whose main job is to play in the middle of the ice

concussion (kuhn-KUSH-uhn)—an injury to the brain caused by a hard blow to the head

draft (DRAFT)—the process of choosing a person to join a sports team

points (POINTZ)—a player's total goals plus assists

rookie (RUK-ee)—a first-year player

READ MORE

Labrecque, Ellen. *Pittsburgh Penguins.* Mankato, Minn.: Child's World, 2011.

Roza, Greg. *Sidney Crosby.* Today's Sports Greats. New York: Gareth Stevens Pub., 2011.

INTERNET SITES

FactHound offers a safe, fun way to find Internet sites related to this book. All of the sites on FactHound have been researched by our staff.

Here's all you do:

Visit *www.facthound.com*

Type in this code: 9781429676847

 Check out projects, games and lots more at
www.capstonekids.com

INDEX